The Shy Mirror

poems by

Gordon Robert Sabatier

1944-2010

The Shy Mirror
Gordon Robert Sabatier

Photograph of G. R. Sabatier from Tulane University Yearbook, courtesy of William Sabatier.
Front photograph taken by G. R. Sabatier, courtesy of William Sabatier.
Book design by Bill Lavender.

ISBN 978-1-883275-26-6

http://www.xula.edu/review

The Shy Mirror

Foreword: Gordon Robert Sabatier, An Appreciation 　　Darrell Bourque	ix
"The shy, discolored mirror"	15
"In our carnival argument"	16
"Street-hearts"	17
"Dusk"	18
Midnight, City, Spring Tree	19
"Up to bite"	20
"On an overcast Christmas"	21
"The good gift"	22
"Hot-and-cold-headed birds"	23
"Leaves cloud the singleton sun"	25
"When new leaves break open"	26
"What I know of love"	27
"For breakfast, sun honey"	28
"A network of bead-budded twigs"	29
"The swallow cleaves the air"	30
"Snowflakes are the souls"	31
"So far from the Sea"	32
"Wild and manifold"	33
"Crepe myrtle flowers"	34
"When the mockingbird stops"	35
"The mockingbird drops"	36
"Does it take a bird's wing"	37
"The rain"	38
"A Cardinal flamed"	39

Evening Prayer 40

"The red rose yearns for comfort" 41

"The wind in the sand has a dry whine" 42

"Foul and fair" 43

"The poet sits in his shell" 44

"Mainlining joy" 45

"As beautifully" 46

"Fire on the wire" 47

"Live liveoak leaves, like tanks" 48

"My father helped me watch the birds" 50

"Wonder can change" 51

"The rolling laugh of the sea" 52

"You are a tree of lights, my sweet" 53

"Rather than weather in the river" 54

"He heard (or heavened) my prayers" 55

"(Oh, boy) the whale" 56

"If I lived in a tower" 57

"Snow from dark heavens" 59

"This is what the great ones of the eyes" 60

Where My Life Rose 61

"Come here" 62

"Flower, feather, and air" 63

"Twilight, soft brink" 64

"To get to glory you have to go through no-man's land" 65

"The Hallow finds us fallow" 66

"Girl-grain grows into woman green" 67

Song for Music 68

"Lightheadedness in, on, longer waves of water" 70

"Sun on Sheba"   71

Concerning the Cross   72

"Odor of jasmine"   73

For John Ramington, and for His Sister Alice   74

Easter, New Orleans, 1978   75

Clouds and Rogues   76

For a Friend Who Changed His Life   77

Striking Diver   78

"The poor downpour"   79

"My voice is reedy"   80

The Fiddler, in an Hour   81

Today I Spoke with a Friend Who Is a Believer as Yet
    Unbaptized: I Speak of Him in This Poem   83

"Our own hungers call out from the weak"   84

Flowering Pear   85

Looking Back at the Bull and the Bull's Eye   86

"I love the grasses and weeds"   88

God and Mary and Saint Patrick   89

Christmas Season, 1979-80   90

"Pots and pans to be washed"   91

Limits   92

Afterword: *Sunt Lacrimae Rerum*   93
    William Sabatier

Acknowledgments and Editor's Note   97

Foreword: Gordon Robert Sabatier, An Appreciation

Darrell Bourque

There is no singular delight in coming into the world of Gordon Robert Sabatier who is both a natural poet and a learned one too. Almost immediately the reader sees the influences and the echoes of canonical poets. In the poems in *The Shy Mirror* we hear resonance, intended or otherwise, of poets as varied as Emily Dickinson and George Herbert. There is no doubt that this poet knew the works of John Donne and the inimitable odes and sonnets of John Keats, and that in the best ways possible his poems are collaborations and conversations with poets whose works he believed in and loved. In his "other poems" sent to friends, he directly addresses his love for Gerard Manley Hopkins in memory poems. Directly or indirectly his commerce is in the world of poets and poems.

Here is a poet who does what all art asks us to do: to blur the lines between what is human and not human, the lines between pain and ecstasy, between being fully immersed in the physical and the spiritual in the moment of the poem. Here is a poet who uses formalisms we use to harness the fierce and wild. We hear and see the attention to line and syllable in the ways that master technicians pay attention to line and measure and sound and image. But there is more.

Sabatier is thoroughly and completely a New Orleans poet but he is a poet working in a geography that is uncharted as well. He is a Christian poet, a Catholic poet in the deepest sense of the word, but he is never hemmed in by labels or orientations and expectations generated by those labels and tags. It is noteworthy that his one collection, a 15 copy, spiral-bound issue, was created at Christmas time and given as Christmas gifts to his family.

Sabatier is not a mere metaphysical poet, not a mere Catholic poet. He is more the intellectual spiritualist in the mold of Paul Klee, Rainer Maria Rilke, or Marc Chagall. He is the metaphysician whose intense love of the world is the very pathway to the intense love of the indecipherable, the inconceivable, the ineffable and the passionate intensity that leaves art and the poem as the only way to articulate both and mystery and the miracle of the human experience.

When I read these poems I feel as though I am reading more than what we have come to know as *poem.* Sabatier transcends poetry in the ways that the mystics do. When I hear his voice in the poems, I can imagine what it must have been like to be in the company and in the worlds of St. Jerome, the great translator. I hear what I imagine to be the voice of Rumi, the voice of Teresa of Avila, Catherine of Siena, Julian of Norwich, Hildegard of Bingen, or St. John of the Cross. The voice in Sabatier's poems is the voice of prayer, the voice of love of the world as passageway to another world, the voice as a way of breathing and of measuring what is in us and around us, an all-at-once-ness that is not unrelated to the workings of quantum mechanics theories of the universe, an all-at-once-ness where light and matter and energy become the physics of both the universe and the soul of the universe. The god Einstein believed was operative but could not articulate in concrete terms is a god close to the one Sabatier has commerce with, a god Sabatier seems to have the "maths" for, specifically in the way of the poem and in the expression of the poem.

And yet, Sabatier, is a simple poet, an accessible poet. His intention is clear and unaffected. His mission as a poet is humble and even self-effacing at times. He keeps his eye on what he loves: trees, music, sun, prayer, wind, water, God, daylilies, dove, hawk, the mockingbird, jasmine, jazz, grasses, weeds, weather, crepe myrtles and the face of an indwelling God, which he says in one poem is "Scale and Perfume, / and Sweet Salt and Spectrum, / and Righteous Caress."

Gordon Robert Sabatier is a poet who is nearly impossible to categorize, or pigeon hole, or label, but it is easy to know the company he keeps. He is an earnest poet in the way Rabia of Basra is an earnest poet or Hafiz of Shiraz, a dedicated poet as is Thomas Aquinas, a believer poet in the way of Francis of Assisi. To question his authenticity or his worth is to question what makes us artists and musicians and painters and composers in the first place. To even try to place him or rank him with other poets is to assume that one knows what a poem is, wholly and completely. In some worlds such a thing is possible, but not in the world where poets talk to each other and write to each other and for each other.

In *The Complete Works of W. H. Auden: Prose, Volume II: 1939-1948,* Auden writes "A poet is, before anything else, a person who is passionately in love with language." Sabatier might well agree with that assessment of the poet's first preference, but who knows if he might not have launched into a series of poems to show the old master that language is loved thusly because it measures us to ourselves, loved thusly because language is the miraculous link to our breath and our God, to the visible and invisible cities where we live, loved thusly because language articulates the life we have come to know as ours.

Darrell Bourque is a former Louisiana poet laureate and the recipient of the 2014 Louisiana Book Festival Writer Award. He is also the recipient of the 2015 James Rivers Award given by the ULL's Center for Louisiana Studies for promotion of Louisiana arts and culture. His poetry publications include *In Ordinary Light: New and Selected Poems* and *Megan's Guitar and Other Poems from Acadie.* "Where I Waited," a chapbook is forthcoming from Yellow Flag Press and he is completing a full-length manuscript, *Love Bridge.*

The Shy Mirror

The shy, discolored mirror
reveals to us the terror
of uprootings in September:
my face is like a roadmap
but with every line an error.

In our carnival argument,
your tears were the ornament,
your sobs, the movement;
the gaiety, my screams.

Street-hearts
my oak tree sweethearts,
with light-poles under your dresses,
what do I know of your stresses?
What can you tell of my art?
Yellow, nearly-spent light
splays forked on your limbs:
what a waste!
More to catholic hymns and hurrahs
runs my taste.

Dusk,
green light hangs easy-headed
over the street,
in the trees' heads' last glowing.
Their exhaustion is limpid
through thinly-laid dust.
Birds sing, then rest.
Ah, but the trees are still growing!
Clouds frown overhead, before pushing
slowly away.
Soon, I must be going.
Calm evening, calm child.

Midnight, City, Spring Tree

The tree has on its precise negligee
of new spring leaves;
I notice this tonight
more than I did today:
with darkness, intimacy in the city.

From a pole
the blue-white street light
shows through thin and incomplete green covering:
brown trunk, brown limbs.

But not even the most ingenuous child
could cry out "naked,"
nor could its elders think "indecent,"
about this common middle-of-the-night gentility
that gives me so much joy.

You know, some of the same elements
that once pulsed hot and quick in you and me
now flow and react, given changes of life,
thinly and coolly in the softly hissing leaves.
Trees mate without touching . . .

I shall remember your scent most truly,
O delicate distant midnight tree.

Up to bite
like two daisies,
down to struggle
like a dream:
they fought like crazies:
I caught two bream.

On an overcast Christmas,
a windy river scatters light
like a grey horse:
"Love me, I shall last"

The good gift
of
a singing of birds

bits of light
on a clouded
Palm Sunday evening

A tender life-oak
is penetrated
flowing with music

more gentle
to the Passionate heart
than all the lifeless stars

Hot-and-cold-headed birds,
swallows and swifts,
slash deep air drifts,
and it hardly hurts;
each cut's as tender
as a new blade of grass works,
but with a catch:
a twist of tail,
a flash of bird-wrist.
And, some nights,
before I drift to sleep,
after a certain sleight
of will and mind,
I let a certain caring
cut me deep,
deeper than the cold cuts,
deeper than the quick
surgery of a graceful movement
of a swallow's or a swift's flight,
and I gather my friends' names
in the white nest of my sheets,
under my heart's wings,
and let them ascend
one by one
in my prayers:
a witness,
a lightness . . .

with morning,
birdsong.

Leaves cloud the singleton sun,
but some light shafts pierce through —
more than one.
My own view obscures with sin,
but Love gains access to it
and clears it. Love, afresh, begins.
I remember a face, your face:
how shining it is!
I remember sharing love after pining.
O walking from this needled shade,
stepping into light!

When new leaves break open
their souling, sailing struggle,
smacking with the rain's lips,
they come out light-green
from the bud's huddle and cuddle;
and though tied to hairy and delving roots
that plumb and suckle,
they slender past muddle;
each separate, each subtle.

A rigolette crown
in the spring wind's railing
downsummer they get thicker
and a heavier green,
to the sunhammer's nailing;
and though downfall they sometimes
skin blood,
or a golden past brailling,
downwinter they slip
to a brown puddle.

What I know of love
comes from the trees:
in the silent shift,
light strikes them in the winter
breeding sight-transcending memories.
Though in the greener seasons
light means photosynthesis
and other breeding, please;
I sing around the incidental gift
of the secret season:
the way light visits with
those armstretched, wooden stones.

For breakfast, sun honey;
an air-sandwich, with street smells, for lunch:
a little fresh rain in the afternoon,
and a deep breath for supper;
and, later at night, a few crisp frosty stars:
good, yes; but don't call it high livin'.

A network of bead-budded twigs
against a grey sky:
they breathe, they live.
A life-net for cold winter souls —
though it scratches perhaps —
a map of spring's roads
for the frail and the shy
(be still — nerves explode),
a delicate ladder leading to God
(at the climax, green fire).

"You are worth more than many sparrows" — Jesus

The swallow cleaves the air —
his high home.
Oh, how he divides it around him:
smoothly in his floating,
stirringly in his wingbeating,
his clean ways piercing, defeating, our gloating.
May the sight of his trim coasting
humble all of our high riding and boasting;
but let it not put us to shame:
for man is not mere man
since Christ has come.

Snowflakes are the souls
of water that has died of cold.
What a death!
(What a Resurrection.)

So far from the Sea,
a bird hies him home.
The cardinals gather in the thunder.
Hidden by the storm of our brains
is a Rose.
It guides us through the darkness
by its odor,
and shows us the color
of Living Blood
when Morning,
clearing,
claps its hands.

Wild and manifold —
and yet close up, clear —
the rain's hair,
long and straight,
sea-shells and sisters
a child's longing,
Here.
In the hurt, it is heard;
in the open skin and eye, felt;
a shadow of a long, long word
that the closed heart stumbles on,
but the young
breathes the cool of,
and the comfort.
And when the rain stops,
the child starts again
the long, bright toddle
through senses, yet past them.

Crepe myrtle flowers,
rhumba-colored,
dance above their girdles
in the muggy summer breeze.
I am at ease;
they are pink, white, and purple.

When the mockingbird stops,
I listen to the silence he leaves,
When he calls again,
He balances in it.
And, after he has sung off,
To rest and/or sleep,
I remember him.
I have hope of future song

The mockingbird drops,
in-and-out-ing with his wings;
he slips, he catches himself:
again;
again;
until, at the turning point
he soars up
to rest in a delicate tree
which welcomes him.
A bird: a life.

Does it take a bird's wing
to bring you to love?
Or a sharp knife,
heart-deep?
Or a cruel tongue,
twisted wrong?
O must you look upon the young?

The rain
comes through the woods
with many voices
whispering faintly:
the woods
come through the rain

A Cardinal flamed
in a bare tree,
Easter Sunday evening,
before a heavy rain,
God knows his truest name.

Evening Prayer

In the heartfelt sky
a bird enters the cloister
Lord, I have eaten and drunk
so much
that I am dry —
O God, send my soul moisture.
A pigeon watches and rests
on a telephone wire.
O God, keep watch over
my hatching desire —
do not let me fly off after idols.
Lord, sin is torture —
I shall huddle in your heart —
take my idle fancy
and turn it to vitals.

The red rose yearns for comfort;
the white rose, for storm.
O the white rose is wild and pure:
the red rose is warm.
But I offer a yellow, blown rose,
with a touch of the flesh in its scent,
for the love of those whom I sent away,
and the true love I feared.

The wind in the sand has a dry whine;
the surf cries out of the Cross;
and the inbred depths,
where the wild fish slips,
pearl to us with jeweled songs
sung by salty and foreign lips
until the Word calls
and our thirst drips.

Foul and fair,
insects tear
small eddies
in the scarlet
and polluted air:
beautiful and unaware;
consuming and being consumed
with shiny, and painful, and automatic prayer:
bare wasp, and honeybee covered with hair;
carrion fly,
spare dragonfly,
and Monarch Butterfly now so rare.
Dare what they do,
mankind shall do more than they dare
(foul . . . and fair).

The poet sits in his shell,
eating sand
with the smell of the juice
of storm.
Go into the larger world
following the whorl
of an Infinite Heart,
crossed and crowned
with thorns and flame.

Mainlining joy —
not with a needle
nor on a railroad track —
but a little boy,
whirling from known,
to future, Love.

As beautifully
as the sea shines,
Sally shines.
The sea's face is opaque,
except at the right angle
or quite close up.
Sally's face is sometimes bright,
though often closed to me with clouds
 . . . but sometimes, but sometimes radiant!
Dare I guess at her depths?
Well, I am patient.
 . . . Here I sleep . . .
Eyes can pattern darkness
into a rich forest.
 . . . Here I waken,
and cry out, seeing
leaves and limbs of a single fall tree
move across the face of the grey midnight sky
like moths, or snowflakes,
or a school of minnows
(birds? no, more gentle).
It was that beautiful.
Doubtless.
Doubtless.

Fire on the wire
a fish on the hook
silver as a shout in puberty
and deeding blood desperately
from a receptive mouth
gilled as an early fetus
but with more teeth
maturer at death
leaving a red liquid
to diffuse in waters
so blue with lovely metaphor
and tinseling reflexive light
from a yellow star's fire . . .
Can't breathe . . .

Live liveoak leaves, like tanks,
(thanks)
storm my window with light,
bonny blue-white,
glancing off their backs.
The facts: natch.
How many ?
Too many to count.
All right ?
At length, though it bites,
my pain does not hold up
against the storm of such — of all —
beauty, which mounts, mounts up.
It is dark, outside, when I go look.
The pane is cold to touch.
It is Advent, New Orleans, December ninth.
Dark-green liveoak leaves, like sleek frogs,
hold both croaks and jumps.
I guess they breathe.
When they fall in the rains, they will be brown frogs dead.
We are tongue-biting toads
covered with bumps.
When we see ourselves as such,
or as we are,
we can seek and behold
beauty of the fly
or as it lies asleep,

not to be touched.
But . . .
Don't rush me please.
But,
when He, She, It . . . Beauty . . . is to be touched,
to be tasted, in love;
let the four winds blow
and the nations rave,
no matter,
we shall be merry
from such fusions and feastings,
and long after;
both merry and grave.

My father helped me watch the birds
and I watched my mother in the flowers
in the summer,
              in the evening,
                      when I was very young.
And I said again the words
to my brothers
and to others.
But long before I knew to tell
a robin from a towhee
or a lily of the Day
from one of the Tiger,
I knew Love,
foreshadowing all flower-fragrance
burning in the manner
of a swallow in transport
shining forth and singing
in my family and friends.

Wonder can change
the process of the heart
into a precess;
like vibrant children, whirling,
during recess.

The rolling laugh of the sea:
wallow-water,
tart fish,
water-breasting mother whales,
mermaid oyster,
sea-slugs,
great big mollusks,
starry plankton,
lush algae . . .
but grave sharks always pacing back and forth;
and the land hidden, milked over, as eyes by cataracts;
and the terrible secret-making-and-keeping sound
of the wind unweaving, unwearying.
Be wary of the grey-irised eyes that suck unfearing,
so shallowly marrying the catch of despair.
O sea: salty grandmother of writer's ink, tears, blood, and
      so forth
Two-legged land mermaids are more dangerous than the
      sea-scaly,
than the sea-fair.

You are a tree of lights, my sweet:
deep as the family of starlight,
yet like a star-map, neat.
I would land a meteorite at your feet.

You are a tree of leaves, my love:
I remember your clothes as being green;
I remember your hair as leaves with an autumn laugh.
I never saw you with either off.

You are a tree of flesh, my lush.
Do not think me rude; flesh is, or can be,
good to behold and touch — remembering the starling
    soul
and the heart that knocks like a thrush.

O starry, leafy, animate Wood,
anointed with words perhaps fresh,
accompany me to my dwelling-place
where we hush, and cherish breath.

Rather than weather in the river,
angered and tethered, a buoy;
or wither in a unstruck bell,
buried years ago, deeper
than sea-sowing or smell's privilege;
or preen and burgeon selfish
in the prim plum of this
merely technical virginity
that surges and smirches habitually;
or plumb gnomish and howlingly
in the depths of all that should not
even be named;
rather than these,
I would ride with the wind's body gently,
explored and exploringly,
and chime out the news that Easter
came truly, and comes forever.

He heard (or *heavened*) my prayers,
despite my holy airs,
did Christ the man in flesh with us —
even in our fuss and goings-on
that come from our flesh not being free
until after death;
death with the attic,
though not with Cybele
(here I mean the Phrygian one
not the modern child of my modern friends).
I have striven too long to understand too well
everything I say or write;
bully, bully: bloody, bloody: quite, quite;
muddy . . . and suddenly clear.

(Oh, boy) the whale
buoyed up by its fat
sings in the depths
like a deep-voiced
prosperous child
in his bath.
God knows what form
their chanting will take
after the Sea is no more.

If I lived in a tower
and the birds flew over —
dove, hawk, and mocker —
I would still be a lover of beautiful
bestowable words,
and a drunk talker.

If I lived in a tent
on the edge of the forest
or in its center
I would not blink
at the harvest that rose
to be gathered
from the dark storm-chest
around the conduits
where hot and cold fluids
torrent past each other —
breath and the rest —
and such a bother
for thicker stuffs
as well as brain-water;
nor would I fear the false words of druids.

If I lived victorious
by sea-water
and the whales rolled over
to be rubbed on their bellies

and the porpoises shrugged and fawned,
and the sea-birds
yelled and shrieked like fiddles,
and yawed and yawned for morsels,
and the wave-crests and wind
shook drops of applause at my feet,
I would not throw my pearls again
to those without taste
though they strain to put out
the rights of our inner eyes.

But I live in New Orleans,
where the bars stay open
and the girls look good
and poetry is understood often
and fitting praise is given
to the One who is Lord
who is Scale and Perfume,
and Sweet Salt, and Spectrum,
and Righteous Caress.
I pray for conversion.
I pray for the Prize.

Snow from dark heavens
has no need of leavening
as it mounts in this town,
piling up better than the rain;
and within, more silence.

In New Orleans, more than three years since such scenes;
yet I grow strong in my greens,
overcome muddy blues,
and pour fluids into my leaden look
with the license we have,
written in red (though perhaps we misapply it).

But Oh, for less humidity on these hot July days,
for more coolness in bed!
Here let me tone down the blood, my loud blood
amid this sweat that stinks so much —
here I do not exaggerate —
here let us hook up to God.

. . .

Grace is like that snow in New Orleans
or other such poem:
it cools off our cramp,
comes freely, though we can ask;
it is delicious in play,
and carries promise of victory
over even a mortal wound.

This is what the great ones of the eyes
have left us:
that leaves under light
(of sky or of lamp)
love us with, and love with us in,
the language of the very stars,
and leach the tracks of those shining ones
like flowers warm the sunbeams from our eyes.

Where My Life Rose

The hills where my life rose were thunderheads
growing up ever so much bolder than the man-bled
    meadows —
child-bleeding then, later seen green —
though neither was as weird as the rivers and lakes
from which fish gurgled to us secrets about death
that lightning threatened and taught me to pray by;
and the good-natured earth choked with slaughter,
but gritted its teeth, as the Second World War sent mycelia
    underfoot
and fairy-tales' rings obscured the growth of faith;
and my father came home from his strange battle with
    others' wounds,
and went on with it, making them his own to some extent,
and still does I think;
and the war-waging moon lit, *lights*, up the naked towns at
    night.
Back then I never knew anyone who had lost his life,
But yet, we knew a bit, a bite, of war.

Come here
said the summer
while it was still spring:
and I went there,
dumber than laughter,
laughing.

Flower, feather, and air;
I saw Him
humming there.

Twilight, soft brink,
when upstairs swallows and nighthawks
beat and slant-slight the air for insects, with some deaths,
and curtains open to the other stars . . . burning bright
    eyes.
Hearts — our hearts — catch fire like this.

To get to glory you have to go through no-man's land:
hop up, then, and over the barbed-wire tightrope;
then dodge-work on the slopes for agony
until you know it's useless;
then picking up oscillations of hope
at the bodies of the fallen,
as bats and bullets fly past like ghosts whistling;
then staggering around with your own screams until you
    nearly faint;
then receiving the insults nobly:
the ones like tomatoes,
the ones like pining peoples' apples and cones,
and the well-aimed slingshooter-shot pieces of dried-up
    shit;
then the moats, wealthy with feces and corpses,
into which you stumble and are purified by:
until now the enemy has not dared to show his face, or
    what
he claims is that —
when he does, seek the face
of the indwelling God,
or look for His face in a comrade,
or consider all the pearls and rubies
among which you have passed . . .
and become as bright as a party-pomegranate
in generosity, and a lily-bud
which is going to — always a surprise — explode.

The Hallow finds us fallow,
bids us follow (the plow).
He would give us food and drink
to fill our hollowness;
He would give us seed to sow,
in his kindness.
And we rejoice, crying out;
"Come, let us do so, and follow . . ."
But we doubt:
"O God, how?
for I am so low."
We confess, we sorrow —
still, "How?" we say.
He tells us:
"I know you thru and thoro.
Taste, know the One you bless.
Embrace Him in His Whole-and-Holiness!
Rejoice in His Kiss of Blood, Soul, and Flesh, afresh!
Chew, sip, and swallow."

Girl-grain grows into woman green,
threshes with pain,
then goes grey into crone;
and then the end.
And that's my own, my Mary Lou,
and the wives of all my friends:
start out little shy buds, blossom into tart coquettes,
then wed-wives and true mothers, save a few;
and they work like mules for years;
it wears them out;
though at times they crow like languishing hens,
or raven stiff and mute, with the hard old stones.
One knows this better than the nuns;
nuns know this better than I do.
"Hold it!" you say, "That's your joke;
that's your angle; that's your dumb-bell jingle-jangle;
but where's my payoff for reading this?"
— Oh, I wasn't through.
Do as I here say:
take up your yokes of rosaries,
and, like the bees, live out your prayers;
you shall flash brighter than the flowers and spring leaves;
sweeter than the blushing pears
shall be your mouths' nectar.

Song for Music

The seasons whiz by so fast
There's hardly enough time for breath.
A couple blew me kisses — two —
from their train to happiness;
on their way to a happy death.

I saw her in the rain,
standing on the bridge.
O she was taking pictures there;
'twas there I made my pitch
I said we'd strike it rich.

They sported in the sun,
their bodies quick and strong.
If we had known we'd age so soon,
how solemn we'd have grown,
how silent we'd have been.

We chatted in the lounge
while waiting for his flight.
I said, "My friend, I think you're wrong."
He said, "I know I'm right."
He took off in the night.

Do you see that little bird,
dancing in the wind?
We cannot know, but I hope, though,

that that's the way I go.
La la, la la la la.

Lightheadedness in, on, longer waves of water.
Whitecaps pass quickly, falling over,
Yet their curls are not lost.
The shark cannot be criminal,
Nor can the dark and depth-plumbing rays.
Though their voices are strange,
Whales wail innocently and porpoises play without malice.
None of the above are indebted to us.
A girl who held me to Christ
wore a wild face.
I drank from her eyes and shaved myself close.
She was as unconquerable as truth.

Sun on Sheba,
in the cane field.
Were I Solomon,
you'd know more about her.
But I can tell you:
she's a girl
somewhere in South Louisiana
and I haven't yet found her out.

Concerning the Cross

Lord, your cross
must have hurt your whole body,
including your sex.
We'd call that the height
of your passion — correct?
Or was the worst
the fire, finally,
in your heart and head?
Did you, did you feel any anger at these —
or embarrassment?
I shall be your cross-patch madman now;
God knows how far I must go:
deeper, I fear, than the winter
of dead summer.
But O may the starlings dally
over my grave
if it comes to that:
may the egrets' frost
recall me in their flights
if it be merely this.

Odor of jasmine
every spring,
for hotblood and has-been,
and all-in-between.
I breathe it in like a madman,
then exhale like a sad jazzman unseeing.

For John Ramington, and for His Sister Alice

When He of Rain and She of Wind
wrangle and tinkle, dingle-dim,
and dangle down deathless, so slim
through tentative, dauntless April
when new leaves still sing promises
and the slow rose's full kiss has
not yet swollen to be given to them;
but the trees are newly-muicy,
child-skinned, ragged Andys and Anns;
would it be intellectual
honesty to question: whether
the Weather and Strange Whim might not
some day in guillotinery
come down hard and stop this; and whether
sap, and leaf, and flower, and Jane
(and June), and Ann, and Alice, and Jim,
(and August, and even July)
might be put to a finish, and end?
O, O: two "O"'s — one for each half
of each grey-green couple in Spring
who live for trysts, wrists, and kissing.
But Ah, Ah, Ah; for the Trinity
who would have us rest in His Bosom.

Easter, New Orleans, 1978

Swallows: feathered fellows and girls
Shrugging and curbing in the easy air
of Easter evening —
not a curl of smoke in their roundabouts — nor sparks.
What they do, they do expertly to eat:
A feast taken lightly, to other birds' shouts —
whose voices in feathers hide out in and among
the live-oaks' new leaves and love-locks.
We are quiet, our cloth is faded, our bones are too large;
but this day, of all days, we need not feel any lack
at flight-grace, bud-bloom, or giftedness in song —
though perhaps we feel awed.
Nothing we touch is Unclean to us, nor
are we as lowly as the highest mere bird;
our souls are, and know they are, more noble than before:
a feat done by you more than masterfully: ah, Lord that you are.

Clouds and Rogues

Thank you, Lord, for clouds and rogues.
Some folks would say to thank you only for the first.
But I give you thanks for both.
For clouds:
all shades from white to black,
toward night blessed-off, back-lit,
with hidden heart and edged with gold.
They are born to bloom and burst.
They grow in a day like stories.
They serve as breasts for the upper air.
They tender-thunder the middle of the night for those
who sleep alone.
They are underslung by nobly-gesturing birds.
And for those who sleep with company, the sight of one's
good friend or mate by lightning!
I thank you also for the rogues.
I don't mean to say that they can have no hope.
I have hope, and I can play the rake, the brute, the bozo.
They let us know — more so than the just, sometimes,
that we must always seek you.
One made me glad for clouds, this evening.

For a Friend Who Changed His Life

That's Charley's voice in the distance . . .
do you remember him?

No.

He gave the girls the bittersweet,
And he was very slim.

Oh, yes, the one with the starving looks
who talked as if he were singing.
Sang me a song once and his eyes were as black
as dark diamonds. What's he become?

He's turned into a poet, now . . . he sounds
real tired when he's not smiling,
with his eyes lit up by fire.

Striking Diver

Down-dog a blitz, striking diver,
goes the nighthawk in his evening streaks:
long-winged, a dark bird in bright fits.
He climbs up, dries out, darts down
with his large mouth dealing death:
zip, zap: he flies, he cats.
His feats feed *us* in the needs of our wits
in this wilderness of crossing, prisoning streets
where we go half in terror, half-asleep,
and long, still, to hear or see
that which dashes and surges and flies free.

The poor downpour —
"spent all my money
and got to go home" —
down air,
downstream to the sea —
salty and slimy and square with fish.

My voice is reedy,
But, when I am moved to, I sing.
I sing for the needy,
to whom I belong;
I sing for the greedy,
who say that I'm seedy
and that I sing a fool's song.
Won't you, won't you, won't you — please — sing along?

The Fiddler, in an Hour

The fiddler, in an hour,
tickled our humor,
trickled out our sorrow
                    like a razor blade,
tensed the gut,
                        stirred up the heart
with strokes of pride and valor:
we'd fight anybody, then, together,
like the brave folk — our close kin — so high in our
    regard:
we hoped we'd be as brave as they had been;
we thought that we were much like them.
There were other songs, as well, that we enjoyed;
but with a certain few, he almost broke our breath;
smothering our breathing,
tightening our chests,
with the back honey of autumn,
with the kind chains of spring,
he violined . . .
of a place where men and woman
whom we were not so much like
could eat, drink, love and suffer,
alone and together, in their lives,

and not be ashamed of each other, or of themselves.
It ended, I think, with a jig: we all stood up.
A fiddler can play to a man's core.
That's why we looked away — or wished we could — that
    hour.

Today I Spoke with a Friend Who Is a Believer as Yet Unbaptized: I Speak of Him in This Poem

A man — about my age — with eyes
like dawns beside the Gulf,
told me, in a bar, that his wife,
a year ago, had cuckolded him and had cast him off.
He spoke of this with no bitterness
nor pride
nor demand for sympathy,
but, rather, like the Christ,
Who, having risen from the dead,
exhibited His healed wounds, of extremities and side,
to a man who had not known or suspected
what Love can do, *will* do,
to comfort and restore
those cast down by selfishness and by treachery.
A woman had beggared my friend like a fallen leaf
and had made him as one blind;
another woman, fresh as grass,
had come to his relief and rescue.
Love will find worth in all that God has wrought or wills;
Love, God's name and gift, makes all things new.

Our own hungers call out from the weak,
and we who trust in our strength
should be softened by their eyes and their speech,
as the air softens light;
we must give them warmth, and to drink, and to eat.

Flowering Pear

A flowering pear,
listening,
growing there
in the back yard of my neighbor.
Covered with white blossoms
and darker green leaves.
In the middle of my life,
through rain
and stirring air,
I saw it.
Cheer into flowering.

Looking Back at the Bull and the Bull's Eye

One Sunday afternoon in our tense
while visiting the country,
we went into the somewhat-dangerous pasture
of a great Brahma Bull
owned by a man not his master,
in order to tease from that beast
some response or answer
to questionings that this nature
presented to us.
His bulk, force and peace
accused our self-esteemed intellects
of vanity: that brute seemed content
and more dignified than we,
despite his alleged stupidity
and what we wanted to call his ignorance.
The massiveness of his genitals
made ours and those of our best-hung friends
seem small and weak by comparison.
We were all in love with danger then,
not being in love, yet, with men or women;
too much taken with our own novelty
we cared less than we ought to have
for Goodness, Truth, and Beauty (the last
in that list), we were afraid of, especially).
What I want to tell you about, now, is this:
His eyes, as he watched our approach,
were big and suspicious,

but there was no appearance
of hatred or malice or wish to give offense.
His eyes, I later thought to myself,
were moist and soft, and almost as vulnerable
as those of the decorous and proud (short and tall)
mostly Protestant girls — so loveable —
with whom we went to school.

I love the grasses and weeds
in the gold sunlight on the levee.
Many and many a flowering jade
whose name I never knew
appears before me,
bursting with seed
slight and heavy
in September paradox;
in meager soil,
amid granite chunks,
and sustained by the gold-admitting air,
there by the waters of the Mississippi
going downhill to the salt.

God and Mary and Saint Patrick

Green leaves mask the sky, translucently.
I walk under and by, thinking of a glory
Half-bid by green membranes
(a kind by another, a kindness by another).
My ribs remember women:
left side, half-way down, slight pains.
Don't ask me why.
Overhead, blue and white (whitish blues, bluish whites),
just turning grey and rosy.
I pass a woman who is near full term.
I look, for a change, at objects more heavy.
"God and Mary and . . . and all good green things," say the
    leaves,
all green . . . *This* is South Louisiana, mid-September,
near the end of the second millennium, *Anno Domini.*
Green bursts shake my senses, from all sides:
sights, smells, taste-memories (all bitter).
When up comes Allison Cross, my beautiful neighbor;
We talk.
I give her a heart-shaped orange leaf.
She gives me a green one, same shape, right after.

Christmas Season, 1979-80

Two flames.
    I hold your hand.

It is the season of death.
    Though apart, we are not yet departed.

I let my eyes rove;
    They flash on an "F."

"F," for me, stands for failure;
    "if," for resplendent possibility.

It is the season of birth.

My lungs hug each breath
    before taking more.

Tree-buds prepare
    their alleluias for tomorrow.

Water beads refract and distill
    the waning light,

for me, apparently,
    just in joy to sing, and to sing.

Pots and pans to be washed,
la la la la.
Pots and pans to be washed,
la la la la.
It's fun if you do it for somebody else,
la la la.
Do it for Christ,
la la la la la.

Limits

If I could fly as well as sing,
why, dance a jingle-jingle-jing.
Sing a single jingle-jangle-jang,
if I could sing as well as fly.
But neither can I; neither can I.

But as I have ear and as I have eye,
mute me up and lame me down
and sing a single songle sound,
and I'll just look and hear around.
Sing a little bit, and dance profound.

If I go deaf and if I go blind,
there are single songle songs to hear,
and wake me up and spin me round,
light behind the dark around;
and You my Dear.

Afterword: *Sunt Lacrimae Rerum*

William Sabatier

Gordon Robert Sabatier — our Robby, your Bob — was born January 28, 1944 in New Orleans at Southern Baptist Memorial Hospital on Napoleon Avenue. He was the slightly premature first-born of Barbara Ann Joseph Sabatier and Joseph Adolphe Sabatier Jr., MD, who had been introduced through friends and relatives at Tulane University, before the country went to World War II. Barbara became a Navy ensign after graduating from Newcomb, Joe a U. S. Army doctor, a captain, whose Tulane Med. School class of 1938 were conscripted as a unit to Fort Benning, GA, and then overseas. Soon our mother became pregnant with Robby. A war baby, Robby was brought up by our grandparents as much as he was by my mother until our father came back from WWII and the family moved to Baton Rouge. Overseas father, distant father, strange father, who had to get to know him and whom he had to get to know, while being torn apart from Grandpa, Leon Joseph of 1109 Fern Street, the surrogate father, if you will.

Also there were my mother's younger brothers Gordon Joseph, who became a businessman and Leon Joseph Jr., who became an obstetrician/ gynecologist. There were also aunts, Joyce and Dorothy, who became a social worker and a pediatrician, respectively. Grandma, Louise Garrot Joseph, presided over this crowd. These were smart, healthy, good folks. When she was only 10 years old, my mother took an IQ test and scored the highest of "all the public school girls in the city of New Orleans," according to her teacher. She along with her sisters all had full scholarships to Newcomb College. Our father was smart, too. Both his high school and college physics teachers singled him out to help teach the class or at least to help set up demonstrations of experiments. In the Army, he was chief of neurosurgery at the 24th General Hospital in Florence, at the ripe old age of 31. Joe's brothers and sister were all very intelligent people, too. Going generations back, on both sides, the ranks were filled with teachers, doctors, successful businessmen, in south

Louisiana. Robby was named after my mother's uncle Robert Garrot, who had studied sugar chemistry at Harvard and who died of yellow fever in Cuba.

After the Great Depression and World War II, expectations, hopes, and, critically, standards of behavior were quite high for this child, the first grandchild, on one side, almost the first on the other side of the family. It soon was obvious that Robby was very intelligent, curious, active, and he was raised to be more and more so. Aunt Dot, studying to be a pediatrician, would remark all her life how uncanny for so young a child was his fixity of attention; Uncle Gordon gave him copies of *Alice in Wonderland* and *Through the Looking-Glass* when he was five, starting first grade. Robby claimed to have read them before he started second grade. In high school, he memorized pi, as a stunt, to 100 places, that showoff. Why? The tragedy is that nobody, not even my physician father, could recognize Robby was beginning to have a mental breakdown maybe as early as his junior year in high school. Not that there were any good drugs for schizophrenia then that could have "nipped in the bud" that illness.

Robby had been taught, at the "college level," poems, poetry, criticism. He wrote papers, took tests falteringly as mental illness was messing with his mind and brain, but making an honest effort. He was a student in creative writing courses taught at Tulane by Dr. John Husband. I tell you these things to set the record straight for those who would stereotype him as a self-taught, folk, street, "naïve" artist. Behind his antic disposition as fool, clown, madman was a lifetime of reading, study, heartfelt thinking, meditation, and wordplay of all kinds.

He dropped out of Tulane for a spring semester, boarded a Lykes merchant ship to France. Paris is cold and nasty in the spring, so he became lonelier and more mentally ill, though he did get in some sightseeing, drank some wine, ate some onion soup at dawn, went to a prostitute once, and wrote poems. *La vie de bohème.* And pretty soon he came back to New Orleans, was readmitted at Tulane, took more classes but had to be hospitalized at DePaul for about two years, getting worse and worse, then to hospital of the University of Texas in Galveston for shock therapy, and returned to New Orleans about '69, where he lived (not "cured" obviously, but not so crazy he had to be locked up) and tried to go to school and go to work, not lasting in any course of study or job, a heartbreaking descent into Madness and inspiring, albeit all-too-Christlike spiritual, ascent to Holiness. His support system began to fall apart shortly after the deaths of our mother in 1986, his confessor Fr. Harold Cohen later, and his friends Julian, John, Al . . . .

The Shy Mirror was his Christmas gift in 1980 to family and friends. He chose 72 poems out of probably hundreds which he had written, typed them up, and took them to Kinko's to be duplicated and bound, an edition of fewer than 20 copies, as I recall. The title page is inscribed, "For Bill & Susan Ayres, with thanks for the hospitality, Christmastime 1980 (Dec. 23)." Bill Ayres was a friend from Robby's Tulane undergraduate days who had given him a collection of his own poems years earlier. There was a second printing of the book at Kinko's after my brother needed to replace his own copy. The title page of that edition has the earlier inscription lightly crossed over and bears a new inscription, "To the person receiving this, my brother Bill's gift to myself and to you — I gave Bill a copy of this for Christmas in Dec. 1980 — He loaned me that copy to be duplicated — I lost it [his own copy, he meant] & I hope you will enjoy this book."

The next to last time I saw my brother alive was in March of 2010, as he lay dying at the Baton Rouge General Hospital, wrists and ankles restrained to prevent him from pulling out the tubes and wires keeping him alive and kicking. I held up my copy of *The Shy Mirror* and asked, "Is it okay with you if this is published, now?" Although he was proud of the book, had put an obvious, circled "c" for copyright purposes on its title page, and had gone along with our father's earnest but unsuccessful attempt to persuade Pelican Publishing Co., at the time headed by his friend and medical colleague Dr. Milburn Calhoun, to publish the book; ultimately Robby quit trying to get poems published and even asked his good, his best friend Frank Chalona to destroy a sheaf of them, which Frank did not do.

Finally, then, thank you Brandon Taylor Aultman, Robby's sole heir and natural son, adopted at birth, now the owner of the poems, for keeping them safe and letting them be shared with the wider world, in this book, in song, in readings, wherever you want to. Thank you, Ralph Adamo, my favorite living poet and the editor of the *Xavier Review*, for having been my brother's cohort, friend, and honest critic back when you guys and a few others all happened to be working at Tulane's Howard-Tilton Library in the 1970s and would get together to share your creative writings with each other. Thank you, again, Ralph, for featuring his poems in *Xavier Review* 31.2, fall/winter 2011 which issue we treasure, not least for your sincere, measured introductions, so full of heart, intellect, and soul, which I love to read and reread. Professor Nicole Greene, thank you for editing the present volume and giving me this chance to say a few more words about the person who is the most unforgettable character I have ever met, who was my BIG brother and whose KID brother was I.

William Sabatier was born in New Orleans but raised in Baton Rouge. He enrolled at Tulane University, dropped out in 1966 to join the U.S. Navy as an Electronics Technician on destroyers in the western Pacific. He returned to Tulane and graduated in 1972 with a B.A. in French, moved to Boston where he worked in the editorial departments of two academic publishing companies, returned to New Orleans, and started a bookshop, River Books (Broadway and Chestnut), 1975-1981. After a series of clerical jobs in journalism and retail, he became the resident landlord of an apartment house in New Orleans which he and Gordon Robert Sabatier had inherited from their mother in 1986. He is a serious amateur photographer, watercolorist, and the significant other of his dog Rose.

Acknowledgments and Editor's Note

All publications are the result of collaboration among many different people: the writer; his first trusted readers: friends, family, and colleagues perhaps; his editor, copy editor, photographer, cover designer and others. This collection of poems by late New Orleans poet Gordon Robert Sabatier is no different, but because *The Shy Mirror* is a posthumous publication, it has been more dependent than usual upon the efforts of several of Sabatier's devoted readers.

First, I am indebted to my colleague Ralph Adamo, editor of *Xavier Review*, who published a selection of Sabatier's poems in the fall/winter 2011 issue of the journal. Earlier this year, Ralph introduced me to Sabatier's brother William Sabatier who gave me a copy of Sabatier's manuscript *The Shy Mirror,* as well as access to Sabatier's vast collection of photographs from which he and I chose the cover photograph. William has also written a short afterword of his poet brother's life through the lens of his family life, his studies, and his illness.

Before the project could be started, Xavier Review Press needed the permission of the Gordon Robert Sabatier Estate. I am therefore extremely grateful to Sabatier's son, Brandon T. Aultman, who was very receptive to our publication proposal and has entrusted this manuscript to our care. We look forward to future collaborations to publicize his father's writing.

Since the poetry of Robert Sabatier is virtually unknown outside his immediate family and a small circle of New Orleans writers, we wanted to introduce his writing to a larger audience. I sent Darrell Bourque a copy of *The Shy Mirror* and invited him to write an introduction. Having read Sabatier's poetry, he immediately agreed. When Darrell was Louisiana poet laureate, he gave of himself encouraging people to write and read poetry. In helping attract readers to the poems of Gordon Robert Sabatier, he continues in the spirit that imbues both his life as a teacher and as Louisiana's poet. His introduction is an invaluable contribution to this volume.

As always, Xavier Review Press is indebted to Bill Lavender of lavenderink.org for the layout and design of this volume.

Finally a note on the editing of this collection: every effort has been made to remain as faithful as possible to the original. Consistent with the Xavier Review Press style, there have been a few minor changes to Sabatier's original punctuation: "table of contents" has been capitalized and periods and commas placed within quotation marks. Sabatier used a type-writer to create his manuscript, so in the transcription, words that were underlined have been italicized. He always left a space between the last word and the exclamation or question mark. That space has been omitted, but where he left an extra space between one word and another, the original has been retained. The manuscript contained very few typographical errors; when they occurred, they were corrected. Most of the poems are untitled, and in the table of contents, Sabatier placed the first line of the poem in quotation marks; that format has been retained.

Nicole Pepinster Greene
Executive Editor, Xavier Review Press
April 2016